Transform...
BEYOND THE BREAK

by
Starr Baynes Merritt

G

COOPER LEGACY
PUBLISHING

Transform...Beyond the Break
Copyright © 2016 by Starr B. Merritt

Photographs by: Matthew Notice
Make-Up by: Crystal Britney Irizarry
Spanish Translation by: Lilian Aguilar Quirin

ISBN 978-0-9972789-0-3 (Paperback, English)
ISBN 978-0-9972789-2-7 (ebook, English)
ISBN 978-0-9972789-1-0 (Paperback, Spanish)

Published by: GCooper Legacy Publishing
Stamford, Connectiout

Acknowledgements

The God that I serve: You said if I delight myself in you, you would give me the desires of my heart. Who wouldn't want to serve a God like that? I'm so very grateful on so many levels.

The jewels in my crown, Ja'quori and Asia: It is my deepest pleasure being your mother. You have been the kind of teachers – teachers of Life 101 – that make my world so bright that even when it's dark, I can still see the stars. It is my earnest plea that when experiencing a break, you will dig deep within yourself and use what you have to *Transform*...BEYOND THE BREAK. I love you to pieces.

My big brother, Gary Baynes: You speak; I listen. You spoke this book into existence years before I even gave it a thought. Thank you for believing in me. I love you to life.

My friend and mentor, Rev. Dr. Michael G. Christie: You personified the compass that pointed me toward my excellence through *"Real Talk"* group sessions. Grace and peace truly be multiplied unto you.

My childhood friend, Michelle R. Jones: When I told you about this book in November 2015, you grabbed your pompoms and cheered me all the way to the finish line. Thank you for always being supportive and enthusiastic about my endeavors.

My CTR colleagues: Chris, thank you for the opportunity to learn and serve under your leadership. Carolina, Keisha and Roody, I commend you for doing what you do with so much passion. Thank you for embracing me as part of the team.

Manuscript Reviewers

Dolores Burgess, Devyn Nettingham, and Michelle Jones

I can't thank you enough for your honest, thorough review of my manuscript. All that I do, I do in the spirit of excellence; but you pushed me to another level of excellence.

Miss Dee,
You showed me a larger vision that I had not imagined. The Spanish translation of this book is due to your ability to see beyond the expected. Your wisdom continues to speak into my life and I so appreciate you.

Devyn,
Your enthusiasm and desire for excellence are contagious. When I thought I was done writing, you demanded to know *"What happened next?!"* I laughed as I read your comments because I knew you were right...there was more. You made sure my readers would not be left hanging. We all appreciate you for that.

Michelle,
Your comments and edits added exponentially to the quality of the text and, as a result, to the reader's experience. You know what you know and you're not afraid to share it. I can't wait to see what's next.

From the bottom of my heart I thank you all.

I hope that reading this book gives you as much clarity and courage as it gave me writing it.

It is my expectation that you will be encouraged, enlightened and empowered.

TABLE OF CONTENTS

Chapter One
THE BREAK   1

Chapter Two
IT BEGINS IN THE MIND   7

Chapter Three
SHIPS AND SHORES   15

Chapter Four
YOU'RE WORTH THE RISK   23

Chapter Five
THE MOMENTS   31

Chapter Six
LIFE, LEGACY & LOSS   39

Chapter Seven
THE "HOW"   49

MESSAGE TO THE READER   63

NOTES   65

~ *Chapter One* ~

*T*HE BREAK

Who among us has never experienced a break? Broken trust, a broken promise, a broken relationship, a broken bond, a broken home, a broken dream, a broken spirit, broken faith, or a broken heart? I believe that everyone – no matter who you are or where you're from – has experienced some kind of break.

Unlike a broken promise, dream or relationship, broken bones are more obvious and require immediate, specific attention; this is where the differences end. Whether the break is physical, psychological or emotional, a plan for recovery is paramount if a full and complete healing is to be achieved.

There are several options to choose from when considering recovery from a break: fix it, repair it; or restore it. If the break can't be fixed, repaired or restored, then revamp it; give it a complete overhaul. This means that the *"after"* will be different, but better, than the *"before"*. Your perception of your situation or circumstances will be a better version than what previously existed.

Change happens after a break. If you've ever had a broken ankle, you know that how you function from day-to-day changes. You walk lightly on that ankle so as not to worsen the pain.

An important piece, while also dealing with the change, is your recovery. Depending on the individual and what is broken, recovery time will differ. The same holds true in the case of an emotional break – loss of a loved one, loss of a job, separation from a spouse. Every person is different and each recovery is personal. Nevertheless, change invites itself in through a necessity to cope with the break.

After a break occurs, it's natural to be very careful with that which was broken. In the case of the broken ankle, you might be hesitant to put your full weight on it; in the case of a broken promise you might begin to be more cautious about trusting people; and in the case of a broken heart, you may not allow anyone else the opportunity to even get into the space where this may happen again...at least for a while. The change that happens after a break can have an impact on you and those around you.

When the ankle gets to a certain point in the healing process, your physician tells you that you can resume normal activity. This means functioning at a level that meets most of the needs of your day-to-day life.

Your emotional pain cannot be seen. With emotional pain an x-ray won't show your physician a status. What if you disagree with your physician's assessment? What if you don't feel like you can resume normal activity? What if it still hurts? Do you just give up?

YOUR NEW NORMAL. Whether your break was physical or emotional, chances are it has changed you to some degree. What was normal for you prior to the break may not be normal for you after the break. You may be unfamiliar with this new normal, but you are still the expert on your own life and well-being.

As we journey together through the pages of this book, it is my ultimate objective to introduce you to the fundamentals that will empower you to conquer the challenges of your new normal; and in the process, reveal....*The Most Incredible You.* Armed with this information, you can then begin to...

Transform...BEYOND THE BREAK

PEARLS...

1. Have you experienced a break?

2. Does the thought of that break overwhelm you?

3. Do people around you think you "should be over it"?

See if you can track how the break is impacting your life:

Put a check in the box that most describes your mood at the below points of the day.	Happy/ Excited	Sad/ Anxious	Angry/ Tense	Tired
6 am – 10 am				
10 am – 12 pm				
12 pm – 2 pm				
2 pm – 4 pm				
4 pm – 6 pm				
6 pm – 8 pm				
8 pm – 10 pm				
10 pm – 12 am				
12 am – 2 am				

What pattern(s) do you notice?

_____

_____

_____

_____

_____

_____

_____

_____

_____

_____

_____

_____

_____

_____

_____

_____

_____

_____

_____

_____

_____

~ *Chapter Two* ~

*I*T BEGINS IN THE MIND

O ur behavior is dictated by our thinking. The brain is the coordinating center of sensation and intellectual activity. Transformation involves a change in thinking followed by a change in doing. That's easier said than done. Ask a smoker who wants to quit; or an alcoholic who wants to be sober; or someone whose weight exceeds the "average weight" for their height who desperately wants to lose those excess pounds.

Problems cannot be solved in the same intellectual space that they are created. If we consider that the brain is the most complex part of the human body, then it's easier to understand why we cannot change the way it functions simply by wanting. Very few people can change their behavior overnight but it **is** possible to retrain or restructure the brain – transform your thinking.

> *"You cannot change your destination overnight,*
> *but you can change your direction*
> *overnight."*
> *~ Jim Rohn*

It begins in the mind -- the unconscious mind. The unconscious mind and subsequent speech pattern are like an underwater earthquake and the tidal wave that follows.

The unconscious mind is a powerful force that dictates the words we choose. Words, once spoken, cannot be unspoken or taken back. The wrong words, like a tidal wave, can have an extensive damaging impact.

So how do we call under subjection such a powerful force that has the ability to wreak havoc? First, pay close attention to the words and phrases you choose. Notice how you structure your speech. Learn how to listen to yourself when you speak. Replay conversations in your mind and ask yourself these questions:

1. What words did I choose?
2. Why did I choose those words?
3. What kind of emotional undertone did they have?
4. Were they positive or negative in nature?

Asking yourself these questions will awaken your mind to your speaking routine.

Once you become aware of the words and phrases you use, identify the positive phrases and the negative phrases. Start replacing negative words and phrases with more positive ones. The reason for this step in the transformation of your thinking is to change the way your unconscious mind interprets thoughts.

As you successfully replace the negative with the positive, your reality will begin to shift. The negativity invoked by those common words or phrases you used to use will gradually cease; the positivity will gain momentum and strength.

Another exercise that will aid in the transformation of the mind is F.E.A.R.™ This requires a bit more time and effort. Practicing F.E.A.R. can transform the mind from that problem space to that solution space. The kind of F.E.A.R. I'm proposing isn't that fear that holds us back from believing, from succeeding, from having. The kind of F.E.A.R. I'm proposing will lead to positive, recognizable changes. What F.E.A.R. is this? *Forget Everything And Reboot.* Clear your hard drive (mind) of the unnecessary clutter (negative, unhealthy thoughts) and make room for the upgrade (positive, healthy thoughts).

Bad relationship – insults, put downs, disrespect. **Delete.**

Bully at work – humiliation, underhandedness. **Delete.**

A speech that didn't go the way you wanted or didn't get the response you hoped for. **Delete.**

A business idea that had a weak launch. **Delete.**

People who spend their life being your self-appointed judge casting a negative light on everything you do. **Delete.**

Critics with nothing but negative comments about your beliefs, your dreams, and your choices. **Delete.**

Someone who blames their own failure on your success. **Delete.**

Family members who attack your character because they can't use you as their personal ATM machine. **Delete.**

It hurts when someone who is supposed to be part of our support system attempts to shatter our dreams. It hurts when we trust someone and they abuse that trust. It hurts when a friend – or what we thought was a friend – violates a confidence. It hurts, and *it changes us.*

Have you experienced any of these or other kinds of hurts? Are the hurts keeping you from interacting with others who might be beneficial to your life? Do these hurts interfere with your capacity to connect? Have you stopped believing in yourself? Has your growth – personal and professional – been stunted due to these hurts? Are you feeling defeated? I'm going to let you in on a little secret – just between you and me. Defeat needs permission. You're defeated **only** when you accept defeat as your own.

So now...Reboot -- restart your thinking process. As with computers, rebooting is necessary to recover from errors/erroneous thinking. It gets rid of the "stuff" that slows us down and hinders our growth. Depending on how these hurts have manifested in your life and mind, you will require either a soft reboot or a hard reboot. A soft reboot may be required just to re-align your thinking. A hard reboot will be required to recover from the greatest damage. As the programmer of your own mind, you decide what remains after the reboot. You decide what gets uploaded and what gets discarded.

What stuff stays and what stuff goes? There's some stuff that you've had since you were a little child..."*You're just like your father/mother!*"

Some stuff was given to you by someone from your past..."*You're not good enough; You're not pretty/handsome enough; You're not tall enough; You don't deserve me.*"

> *Imagine this -- you're in a small aircraft, just you and your "stuff". Suddenly, you notice the aircraft is beginning to lose altitude. You're proceeding toward earth at a fast pace. Your "freeze, fight or flight" response kicks in. If you freeze, you will undoubtedly meet with an unfortunate end in about seven minutes. There's nowhere to run, so flight – in this sense – is not an option....ironically. So you choose the only option left -- fight. You want to live, and there's nothing more important in this moment than your survival. You begin throwing things out of the aircraft to get rid of the excess weight. The bottled water; the inflatable rafts (you're nowhere near water); the box filled with gifts that you picked up on your trip for friends and family. The plane's descent begins to slow, but not enough. You're down to your personal treasures, and you must choose what you're willing to part with in order to save your own life. You pause*

for a moment, as is human nature before making a life-altering decision, then you begin hoisting the "stuff" that you've become so accustomed to holding on to. The plane begins to re-gain altitude. You're now in a safe space; no longer in immediate danger. You breathe a sigh of relief.

This experience is not uncommon, although much more dramatic. There are times when we have to make difficult choices for the sake of safety (physical, emotional, and psychological). Some of our "stuff" has practical value, some of our "stuff" has sentimental value, and some of our "stuff" is just clutter (emotional debris, unfounded beliefs, and self-destructive habits).

What "stuff" do you have that's preventing you from personal or professional elevation? Attachments? They can be detached. Guilt? Forgive yourself. Self-criticism? Be kind to yourself. Limiting beliefs? Conquer them. Grudges? Let them go. Bad company? Save your own life. Bad memories? Make peace with them. Starting today make a decision to live your new normal.

When you believe that you have power over your "stuff", only then will you realize that you have the power to transform your own thinking. Change the conversation in your head.

PEARLS...

Beliefs and behaviors stem from experiences, education, faulty logic and fear. The good thing about your mind is you can change it.

Choose to...

♦   Magnify the importance of your achievements rather than minimize them.

♦   Expect the best outcome rather than the worst.

♦   Notice the positive aspects of a situation instead of just the negative.

♦   Abandon "all-or-nothing" thinking by eliminating words like "always" and "never" from your vocabulary.

You will begin to see a change.

~ *Chapter Three* ~

*S*HIPS AND SHORES

Relationships vary and may include family ties, friendships, partnerships and companionships. They are built on a foundation of trust, appreciation and respect. Whether the relationship is personal, professional, or romantic, it requires effort and commitment from all parties involved in order to succeed.

Because the male brain and female brain are made up differently, the way they think, act and process information is different. As a result, they have different strengths and weaknesses. In the broadest sense (and in an effort to avoid stereotyping), men are more about thinking and women are more about feeling – in the broadest sense. That's my disclaimer.

The beginning of a relationship represents the shore. This is where trust, appreciation and respect create a feeling of stability. Ships are meant to travel – to move forward. The further away from the shore that the ship travels, the greater the possibility of encountering rough waters – instability. If the ship is going to be kept afloat, the passengers will need to exercise effort and commitment.

Family Relationship: When children are small, they stay close in proximity to their parents, particularly outside of the home. This is out of necessity so they remain safe. As time goes on and children grow into teenagers...rough waters...instability. It's up to everyone involved to compromise – sometimes to the point of surrender – and accept the changes in the dynamics of the parent/child relationship that occur as children become teenagers.

Friendship (Personal): You meet someone at a social event. Through conversation you realize that you have a lot in common, the same likes and interests. From this interaction you look forward to a friendship that is healthy, encouraging and personally edifying for all parties.

Partnership (Professional): You're looking for a new position. One day after months of searching, you come across a position on one of the job sites. This position looks like it was written based on your resume specifically. You apply for the position online. The very next day you receive an email asking to schedule a phone interview. The phone interview goes tremendously well so you're invited to an in-person interview. All of the required skills and qualifications posted in the job description match your experience.

Companionship (Romantic): Couples grow sometimes out of a friendship; they pay attention to each other and focus on meeting one another's needs. Everything is just so right in this new romantic relationship.

These are all positive interactions. But what if your situation doesn't work out like that? The person you met at the event posts negative comments about "people at the event" on social media. That perfect job description followed by the great interviews turn out to be only 10% of the description. One party to the romantic relationship begins to focus on something or someone else.

What changed? Why couldn't the relationship just stay the way it was -- where it was (on the shore), secure, stable? The further you get away from the shore, the more the view (what you see) changes. You may not be able to see what's ahead, but attending to the little things along the way can mitigate the damage in case of a mishap: a life raft in case the ship is disabled or destroyed; a parachute in case you need to jump; head gear in case you crash.

A ship is always safe at shore
but that is not what
it's built for.
~ Albert Einstein

The simple fact is...you might have been powerless as to how your situation turned out. You may, however, decide what happens next. You had no control over any of those events because they involved the unknown variables of the mind, intent and acts of others. You do, however, have control over your response and behavior -- complete control.

This is one of the many tests you will endure in life. What happens next will be a defining moment for you. Be present in this moment and be intentional about your decisions. Are you going to allow that failed friendship to dictate your future friendships? Are you going to stop looking for a job because that one wasn't as perfect as it was represented to be? Are you going to let that woman or that man rob you of the right to be happy with a companion because of their inability to continue in trust, appreciation and respect?

These are limitations. Don't allow limitations, whether self-imposed or put on you by others, keep you from experiencing the success, joy and peace that you want for yourself. Your past does not determine your future and it is possible to succeed at something at which you previously failed. Failure is not the end of the journey -- it happens just before you reach the next level.

In the meantime, consider what might help you be successful going forward. Ask yourself some important questions:

Am I fulfilled as an individual?

Can I give understanding and appreciation to others?

Do I love myself?

Am I committed to my happiness/peace?

Is my heart focused on the needs of others?

Is my communication open, honest and clear?

Am I friendly/approachable?

Am I patient?

Do I know what it means to be loyal?

Answering yes to these questions will help you to create healthy relationships. That includes family relationships, friendships, partnerships and companionships.

PEARLS...

1. What are some hurtful comments you've heard from someone?

Comment	What was your interpretation?

2. What are some hurtful comments you've said to someone?

Comment	What was your intent?

Whenever you feel upset, it can be a useful exercise to write and analyze:

1. Write out your angry thoughts for about 5 minutes without stopping to evaluate or judge them.

2. At the end of your day, read what you wrote and answer the following questions:

    i. What did I feel at the time?

    ii. Was something else going on with me that made it seem worse than it was?

    iii. What do I feel about it now?

    iv. What actions are in my power to reduce the tension of the situation?

~ Chapter Four ~

You're Worth the Risk

See your goal, plan your path, and believe in yourself. Are you willing to risk failure for the possibility of success? Risks and Rewards are present in every area of life. Family life, work or business life, community life, and even church life. A reward is the compensation or gift one receives for service, effort or achievement. What this says is that something generally must be given or done in order to receive a reward. Companies give employees rewards for years of service. Law enforcement agencies have been known to offer a reward for information that may help solve a case. An individual might offer a reward for help in locating a lost pet.

Rewards are given in exchange for something of value. It's easy to see the value in the tangible things like houses, jewelry and cars. But how do we assign value to the intangible...that which we cannot see or touch? First, let's identify valuable intangibles: self-confidence, self-control, compassion and empathy, just to name a few. All of these are valuable and intangible. What makes them valuable is that although you cannot touch them, you can feel them...and you can also feel the absence of each of them.

These intangibles cannot be counted on a calendar, nor can they be checked off of a list. There's no score card to tally them or judge to rank them. Nevertheless, it is possible to set a goal of realizing these qualities in your life. Every decision that you make – or fail to make – will lead you either closer to or further away from any goal. Change takes time.

The journey to self-confidence, self-control, compassion and empathy requires you to take a look at where you are, get yourself in the right mindset, and commit.

Is there anything that you would like to change about your life? Is there a specific area in which you would like to see a transformation? Is there a small change that you would like to see in yourself that might make a big difference for you as well as for those around you? If your answer is "*Yes*" to any of these questions, please continue reading.

The decision to change or transform is completely up to you. You can point to a calendar and pick any day you wish to begin to change a behavior that will bring about an important change in your life. You can open a book that will expand your knowledge on any subject of your choosing. You can begin a new activity any time you would like. You can begin the process of change or transformation at absolutely any time. It's up to you.

The thought of change can be uncomfortable. The discomfort may cause you to choose to do nothing. You can choose not to pick a day. You can choose not to open a book. You can choose to do nothing. If you choose to go forward with this change or transformation, what is the worst that could happen? Any step you take toward the change or transformation will bring you one step closer. The worst that can happen is that you get closer to your goal. Is that so bad? I think not. Indeed the worst thing that can happen is that you are close enough to the victory to see it, but you choose not to continue toward it. You have the ability to make a choice for yourself that leads to positive, desired change. You have the ability to subtly or radically transform any area in your life and it all begins with the decision.

Has someone told you that you can't do it?

When others try to place limitations on you, whether it's intentional or not, make up in your mind to reject those limitations.   Stamp a big red *"Invalid"* mark on those limitations.   You're not rejecting or invalidating the person...just the limitations.   Also, beware of placing limitations on others.

> *When my daughter was 5 years old she attended summer camp at the YMCA. Part of the camp experience at the "Y" was daily time in the pool. She had always liked playing in water so this was right up her alley.*
>
> *One day when I went to pick her up, she was still in the pool area so I went to the pool to see her in action. She was having a ball playing in the shallow end of the pool, you know, where the 5 year olds should be. When*

she saw me, she knew it was time to go so, as with any child, she wanted to take one more dip.

She shouted to me, "Mommy, look!" She then proceeded to run along the pool until she got to the deep end – 12 feet – then she jumped in. My heart stopped, my mouth dropped and my legs froze. A counselor saw my expression and quickly said to me very calmly, "She's okay, she can swim." Asia rose to the surface with a big smile on her face.

If my permission had been specifically requested, she would not have learned to swim in the deep end. I would not have given permission for anyone to take my baby in the deep end of a pool and let her go. I subconsciously placed limitations on my daughter. Asia never limited herself in or out of the water. She has always been told that she "can" and she has always believed it.

How can we, at this stage in the journey, return to a time when we had no self-limiting beliefs? How do we go back to the time when we could do anything we put our heart and mind to without the fear of failure or ridicule? That may be a challenge. Your mind (and some people) will, no doubt, start reminding you of your failures. You start thinking, *"What if I have good reason to believe that I can't do it?" "What if I tried and failed in the past?" "What if all I've ever been told is 'YOU CAN'T...YOU WON'T...YOU'LL NEVER'?"*

What do you do when the enemy is in your own mind? Just when you've made up your mind to take the first step, the conversation in your head begins:

"If you try that, you'll fail!"

"If you do that, then you'll be worse off!"

"This won't work and you'll be disappointed, and you know how painful that was last time!"

"Who do you think you are?"

"You don't deserve to be happy!"

This chatter in your head amounts to distractions. Instead of allowing these thoughts to dictate your next move, elevate your level of thinking. Remind yourself to use words that are positive and effective. Expose negativity in the conversation and replace it with positivity. *F*orget *E*verything (negative) *A*nd *R*e-boot!

Try this for the next couple of days: Listen to the words you use; examine them carefully; write down phrases that you frequently use. Separate them into two categories (negative and positive). Ask yourself, *"Why did I choose those words?" "Are they positive or negative?" "What kind of emotional undertone do they have?"* Replace the negative phrases with positive ones and watch your reality begin to shift.

Negativity can stand in the way of success. We all want to succeed. The desire to succeed can cause us to focus on our fear of failure not realizing that our focus becomes our fixation. Even though it's in the back of our mind, it haunts us. Don't allow the fear of failure to remain hidden like something waiting to jump out of the darkness and startle you.

Fear of failure is normal; but it doesn't have to be consuming. Let's bring it to the forefront – right now – together. Failure is a disappointment, a malfunction, a break. For each of these 'pauses', there is an opposite possibility. As long as you have possibility, it isn't over. I call them 'pauses' because they are temporary...unless you give up in the pause. Thinking of failure in these terms removes the element of fear. Know that failure is a possibility, but so is success.

When you are faced with failure, embrace it as an opportunity to achieve even greater success. You have now eliminated one way of reaching success; you have not eliminated success itself. Identify any false, limiting beliefs that pop into your head along the way and confront them with what you know to be true – you are one step closer to your success.

Be rational and resilient in the face of failure. Fear of failure is a bully (all talk – in your head). When you stand rather than run, the bully loses its power. Much like the law of conservation of energy, power (like energy) is never 'lost...only transferred from one form to another.' You have the power!

PEARLS...

1. Do you place artificial boundaries around your potential?

2. Does someone else place artificial boundaries around your potential?

3. Does someone use their "concern" for you to tell you that you're not good enough?

4. Are you beginning to believe the criticisms you've heard about your abilities – or lack thereof?

These are limiting beliefs. You don't have to accept them.

- Be aware of the limiting beliefs

- Confront the limiting beliefs

- Engage the limiting beliefs

- Expose the limiting beliefs

Your only true limitations are those you place on yourself.

Examine some of the words and phrases you frequently use and change the negatives to positives:

Words/Phrases	Positive or Negative	Replacement Words/Phrases

~ *Chapter Five* ~

*T*HE MOMENTS

Have you ever arrived at work without the memory of having driven there? I've heard people say they've been driving to that same location for so long that the car knows the way. Driving to work is one of the things we do on automatic pilot.

Thefreedictionary.com defines *automatic pilot* as a state of mind in which one acts without deliberate effort or self-awareness.

Functioning on automatic pilot is how many of us go through the common, ordinary parts of our day. This allows us to perform some of our regular activities without getting mentally tasked. After all, how much deliberate thought does it take to brush our teeth, take a shower and get dressed? Most of us can do these things without thinking through them step-by-step.

Let's look at the steps for brushing our teeth:

1. Take the toothbrush out of the cabinet
2. Take the toothpaste out of the cabinet
3. Remove the cap from the toothpaste
4. Point the open end of the toothpaste to the brush end of the toothbrush

5. Squeeze the toothpaste until the desired amount is on the brush

6. Replace the cap on the toothpaste

7. Brush teeth

8. Rinse

Being on automatic pilot for regular, normal or daily tasks allows us to free our minds for more challenging matters. This is the greatest advantage of automatic pilot.

There are, however, disadvantages to functioning on automatic pilot. One very unfortunate disadvantage is the moments we miss, and therefore, fail to give due thought or consideration.

Several years ago I was in a car accident in which I sustained head trauma. For the year following the accident I experienced migraines, slurred speech, and mini seizures. The migraines landed me in the emergency room with an intravenous (iv) drip until we got them under control. I wasn't aware of the slurred speech until I would say something that made perfect sense to me, and the person to whom I was speaking would look at me with a confused expression and respond..."What?!"

The mini seizures eventually morphed into one big seizure ending in yet, another trip to the emergency room. Through all of this I was on automatic pilot – just getting through each day. I was missing, or dismissing, the signs. At some point during the years that followed, the migraines became fewer and farther apart, my speech was no longer slurred, and the seizures ceased completely.

When I finally noticed these transformations, I was thrilled, to say the least. Having been on automatic pilot, I missed it -- those precious, priceless moments. I want to be present in those moments; moments of victory, moments of triumph and moments of relief.

How many moments have you missed all while on automatic pilot -- moments in the lives of your children, your spouse, family members; moments in your career; moments in your service to others? Everything you do matters to someone, benefits someone, is appreciated by someone...except when it isn't.

There are times when being on automatic pilot is the only way to make it through. Several years ago the company I worked for relocated to another state. Since I was unwilling to relocate with the company, I was faced with searching for new employment. Thankfully, because of the package the company provided, I did not have to rush to find something right away. Nevertheless, as a responsible person and parent, I started looking for a job after a couple months of lounging and then temping. I answered a direct-hire job posting for a major company in Connecticut. From the first interview to the time I was finally hired – three interviews later – four months had lapsed. When I was finally offered the position, I was happy to take it. It was better than nothing. In all honesty, the pay was fair and the expectations were feasible. I had never had a job I didn't love...until that job. What followed were the worst five years of my life. Being in that environment was literally *just* better than nothing.

I learned quickly that whenever substance follows lack, it's human nature to be grateful. There's a feeling of joy and expectation because of the newness of the experience. Because my mind was in a happy place, I questioned my own perception when I heard snide remarks. I wondered to myself on more than one occasion, *"Did she really just say that?"* I questioned my own perception when insults were hurled through the air with seemingly no target. I wondered what I *wasn't* doing when veil threats were thrown in the air at no particular individual, after which you could hear a pin drop. This was a level of rudeness and hostility that I didn't know existed. The discomfort of my co-workers was obvious. They couldn't wait to get me in private and tell me that I was the new target and that this rude hostile perpetrator was now leaving them alone to focus on me. It's unthinkable, but yes - bullying occurs in places you would never imagine.

Don't ever give anyone a reason to believe that you don't have any alternatives outside of them. They may appear nice and shiny on the outside, but if you think you have been verbally abused...you probably have. Trust yourself -- stop talking yourself out of the knowledge of the truth. Recognize manipulation when it's happening to you. If you feel like you're being handled...you probably are. If you feel like you're being controlled...you probably are. If you feel like you're being disrespected...you probably are. Who better to determine this than you? You might think to yourself, *"Well, it's better than nothing."* Maybe, maybe not -- that's for you to decide. The point here is...arm yourself with the truth of your situation and make sure it's **your** decision.

PEARLS...

1. List your top 5 achievements.

     i.

     ii.

     iii.

     iv.

     v.

2. Spend a few minutes each day enjoying the successes you've had.

3. What would others consider to be your strengths and weaknesses and what opportunities and threats might these provide?

	Strengths	Opportunities
i.		
ii.		
iii.		
iv.		
v.		

Weaknesses	Threats
i.	
ii.	
iii.	
iv.	
v.	

Everything you need in order to be *The Most Incredible You* is already inside of you. No one else can do what you are here to do. If you abandon or reject your purpose, you deprive the universe of that which only you can provide.

~ *Chapter Six* ~

*L*IFE, LEGACY & LOSS

In the grand scheme of things life is short. You've heard it said and you've probably said it yourself. But have you ever really given it much thought? What will your legacy be?

As we pulled on to the street, there were cars in every space -- finding an available parking space seemed impossible. We drove up and down side streets until finally, we found a spot a couple blocks away. As we were walking from the car, we noticed the out-of-state license plates: New York, Maryland, Virginia, South Carolina, North Carolina, the list goes on. Wow! This was an amazing sight to see.

*As we approached the building, the crowd was such that people were still waiting to get in. The crowd was very large and gathered close together. In spite of the lack of personal space, there was a feeling of patience and understanding in the atmosphere. Everyone was greeting each other with smiles and hugs. We heard people introducing themselves and indicating how they knew the individual with whom they were speaking. Others were trying to **make** people remember who they were.*

Finally, we made it to the inside of the building; we signed our names, and continued to wait to proceed. The crowd continued up a small set of about five steps to an entryway. Once we breached the shadow of the entryway, the room seemed to open up. There was music playing softly and lots of whispered conversations. There was not a seat available in the place – neither the main area nor the balcony. There were people lined along the walls and even on the stairs to the balcony.

We proceeded at a glacial pace as did the rest of the crowd. As we continued toward the front some, elements began to come into view. Off to the left center in the front was a man facing the crowd. He was wearing what appeared to be a sort of a soldier's garb, an apron (over his suit), and holding a very long sword. This was an armed guard. I had never witnessed anything like this before.

The crowd continued moving slowly toward the front – each person pausing at the front, then proceeding to their right to greet those who were already seated, and then find a spot to sit or stand wherever they could.

As the crowd thinned in front of me, more began to come into my view. Finally, we made it to the front. There he was; my grandfather, Jake Cooper – lying in repose. He had transitioned from earth to Glory and this was his homegoing celebration.

What a life, what a legacy, what a loss.

In the days prior to his transition, my Grandfather was surrounded by family. On the evening before his passing a series of unfortunate events – which I later viewed as very fortunate – created a break in my schedule which allowed me to visit with him. I sat on one side of him, Aunt Sandy sat on the other. When Aunt Sandy finished reading to him, we began to talk. I told her about my memories as a child spending weekends at my Grandfather's house and the fact that he always prepared home-cooked meals for us...no fast food. As we spoke, my Grandfather began to smile. He hadn't been awake in several days but he smiled. Oh what peace.

It was evident on the day of my Grandfather's homegoing that he left a legacy. Not only his children, grandchildren and great-grandchildren – all of whom were fortunate enough to know him – but also his sisters and their children, grandchildren and great-grandchildren; a host of friends and members of the organizations in which he served.

What will your legacy be? What impact will you have on the lives of others? Will you change the conversation in your head if it's negative and unproductive? Will you ask yourself the questions that lead to creating healthy relationships? Will you activate and stir up the power that's inside of you? Will you make decisions that decrease any threat to your well-being?

What will your legacy be? A legacy is money or property passed from the owner to the recipient through a will or trust; it's a gift. A gift is a talent, skill or ability. I've heard it said that a gift is a gift only if it's given away. What will your legacy be?

Even if a great legacy is left, the feeling of loss will have its place. Along with the loss comes the almost certain competing family dynamics. If you've ever experienced a loss in your family, you have probably witnessed some of the fallout that can follow. Families, if not careful, can be destroyed by the events that transpire after a significant loss.

Factual Events Shared by Anonymous Individuals:

> *"My mother passed away several years ago. My brother refused to attend the funeral. Today he still has so much anger and resentment. I believe it's partly because of the choice he made all those years ago. He's distant with my brothers and me and he rarely makes contact. We not only lost our mother, but we also lost a brother."*

> *"When my sister passed away she left a one year old son. She had a will, but my family and I were surprised by what was in it. She gave my younger sister custody of her son. We didn't think the life this sister lived would be*

good for a child. My family and I were so sure she would grant me custody. What a shock. As difficult as it was to accept, it was my sister's wish. Eventually the shock wore off and we were all a support system for my little nephew. He turned out just fine."

The word "loss" most commonly refers to the loss of a loved one who has passed away. In actuality, a loss is a loss whether it comes in the form of the death of a loved one, a relationship that has ended, a job that has been lost, or a pet that has died (or been put down). Loss, in this context, can be explained as the sudden and eternal absence of something or someone.

Recovery from a loss requires the same dedication and commitment as recovery from drinking, smoking or substance abuse. At some point in the process of recovery, forgiveness is usually required. The courage to forgive can seem unthinkable. Forgiveness takes effort. To forgive is one of life's greatest achievements. Forgiving yourself or someone else can be a very difficult road to a very rewarding destination.

Forgiveness, like a little drop of water, has far-reaching implications. Forgiveness spreads beyond ocular boundaries, but what *is* seen is the impact. The confusion and destruction that can plague a family after a loss can be minimized, or even mitigated, if the perpetrator chooses forgiveness over being right, forgiveness over being wronged, forgiveness over getting revenge, forgiveness over all the offenses that – when triggered by events or individuals – serve as a constant, hurtful reminder of the loss.

Dealing with and learning to be with grief is a very personal, individual experience. No one can dictate how long it "should take" to recover from a loss. It's not uncommon for two siblings birthed from the same parents and raised in the same household to have completely different responses to a loss. Neither of them is wrong. The relationship with the person who has transitioned might seem the same, but no two relationships are exactly the same.

You may feel anger. You may have crying fits. You may just feel like screaming. You may feel numb at times. All of these reactions are common. It's okay; you're okay. Allow yourself the time and space to feel what you feel without judging yourself.

It's important to take care of yourself: Listen to your body; Eat something - even if it's a little bit; Shower – it will refresh you. Take your regular medications – it will help avoid physical setbacks. Handle business a little at a time. There will be some immediate concerns, then there will be others that can wait. Do what you can when you can. You will encounter individuals who disagree with how you handle some things. Take a moment, if you can, to listen to and acknowledge their thoughts. Let them know you appreciate their advice, then do what you feel is best.

A colleague of mine, Claire Schwartz, wrote a very insightful book called *"Putting Out The Fire: Nurturing Mind, Body & Spirit in the First Week of Loss"*. In her book Claire shares her own experience with multiple losses as well as how she has learned to cope in the days immediately following.

THEN THERE'S THE LONG-TERM.

Grieving the death of a loved one is very painful and at times can be overwhelming. Individuals often worry if they are grieving "the right way" and question if they are "normal." Grief is not just sadness or depression; it's a whole host of feelings and emotions. Besides affecting your emotions, grief reaches into every part of your life: your work, your relationships with others and your image of yourself.

Everyone grieves differently. There's no single correct way to express the pain, sorrow, yearning, and other aspects of the transition of adjusting to the death of a loved one. Don't allow anyone to make you feel like you're "losing control," when in fact it's simply how you actively (and productively) process the loss.

Some people never cry. Tears are an outward expression of anguish and this isn't everyone's grieving style. This doesn't mean they're grieving less intensely than a visibly shaken individual or that they loved the person who transitioned any less. Nor does a lack of obvious emotion mean the grieving individual has an emotional block or problem or will face a longer, more difficult adjustment to the loss.

Some people never stop grieving a loss; they learn to live with it. Grief is a response, not a straight line with an endpoint. Accepting that death is real (and not your fault) isn't the same as being okay with it. It simply means absorbing the truth of what has happened.

PEARLS...

Grief is a natural response to loss and it can unfold in many ways. There is no "right" or "wrong" way to grieve.

Try not to get caught up in these myths:

Myth #1: It's possible to cry too much.

Myth #2: If you don't cry now, it'll be worse later.

Myth #3: Grief is something you "get over."

Myth #4: Time heals slowly but steadily.

Myth #5: Grieving should end after a set amount of time.

Myths are fairytales – they are not true. Allow yourself the time and space to grieve without judgment. Be kind to yourself even when others don't understand.

~ *Chapter Seven* ~

$\mathcal{T}$HE "HOW"

Promise – your promise is your talent and potential. Passion – your passion is what excites you; that which you desire. Possibilities – your possibilities are options and opportunities. Your promise will give birth to your passion and your passion will lead you to your possibilities. These are the traits and characteristics that help define who you are.

How do you go from your promise to your possibilities? How do you handle detours? How do you deal with the doubts – yours and those of others? What do you do when it looks impossible?

There's no need to sugar coat it;
sugar melts in a storm.
~ Starr Merritt

The Storm...

A neighborhood in the projects – one of the safest and most fun places to grow up in the 70s – where small children were playing outside at a time when children actually played outside. One of the little girls, 5 years old, was hit by a car. The sound of children playing was replaced with gasps and screams from every direction. The car that hit the little girl had been going very fast; it knocked her about 10 feet in the air and she landed on her forehead. When the police arrived at the scene and saw the child, they called off the ambulance. This tiny little girl lay in the road with no skin left on her bloodied forehead. She just laid there as screams turned into screeches. The police took a sheet, as was protocol, and laid it over the little girl...covered her from head to toe. The police pronounced her dead.

While everyone stood around watching, the police were waiting for the coroner. The neighborhood children (and parents by this time) stood there...stunned. This 5 year old little girl that they knew and played with was gone – right before their eyes...the break.

But wait...the sheet moved. The little girl that had been declared dead by the police had moved her hand. Of course, panic ensued. The police, having wasted all of this time, immediately called for an ambulance. Dread turned into hope that day.

That little girl in the street bleeding from her head and covered in a death sheet is now an adult. That little girl has successfully counseled teenagers who faced their own dread. That little girl from the projects today is a published author. That little girl is committed to helping people from all walks of life *Transform*...BEYOND THE BREAK. That little girl is me; living my promise, pursuing my passion and excited about my possibilities.

Has dread entered your life? Has your passion been declared dead? Has someone thrown a death sheet over your promise? Don't just lie down and accept it. Move your hand! Do something! Participate in your circumstances. Move your hand! Defeat needs permission. Don't authorize it.

You have power over your success. How you prepare will determine your effectiveness. Setbacks and obstacles are part of the journey. How you choose to deal with them will determine your outcome. If at any time you don't like the way things are going, you can make a change.

What opportunities are you considering? What is standing in your way? What are you going to do about it? How will you position yourself to get the most out of that opportunity?

Picture, if you will, a group of people gathered in a public location for a common cause. The leader of the movement has a megaphone yelling, *"What do we want!"* and the crowd responds with *"Victory!"* or whatever it is they're fighting for. Then the leader says, *"When do we want it?"* and the crowd responds *"Now!"* This chant continues back and forth for a while...

Leader: What do we want?

Crowd: Victory!

Leader: When do we want it?

Crowd: Now!

The one thing we fail to ask or consider is, *"**HOW** do we want it?"* How do you want to achieve your victory? What will your commitment to this victory look like? When will you take the first step on the journey toward your victory? It's up to you.

Identifying your victory – knowing what you want – is the first step to achieving that victory. This will allow your mind to help you succeed. When your mind and your goal are in synch, you're ready to take deliberate steps toward your goal. If you have a goal but no direction, no progress will be made. Don't live your life as if your goals are a matter of chance. Your goals are a matter of choice.

Pay attention to your progress, celebrate your victories along the way – big and small – and learn from your failures. Know that failure is not final; it's just a deviation – an opportunity to make a course correction – another step toward your victory, but only if you keep moving forward.

When you're faced with having to make a course correction, you have to be willing to change your mind about that original course. If it isn't going as you planned, do something different. Your willingness to do something different will help you overcome the unexpected obstacles. Focus on excellence and don't allow your focus to shift no matter where you are on the journey. Excellence is not perfection; excellence is doing what you do to the best of your ability and doing it better as you progress.

The only way to know you're moving forward is to be aware of your progress each step of the way.

PEARLS...

Visualize yourself at your goal.

In reverse order, list the steps you need to take in order to reach this goal:

1. The step right before reaching your goal:
2. The step right before 1 above:
3. The step right before 2 above:
4. The step right before 3 above:
5. The step right before 4 above:

Who can help you toward your goal and how can they help?

Person	How can they help?

Get started!

~ Just the Beginning ~

*Remember, the only thing you cannot change
is the past.*

Transform...Beyond the Break

Broken trust, a broken promise, a broken relationship, a broken bond, a broken home, a broken dream, a broken spirit, broken faith, or a broken heart? Everyone has experienced some kind of break and I believe it's possible to *Transform*...Beyond the Break.

Transformation involves a change in thinking followed by a change in doing. Start by using F.E.A.R.™. Ask yourself the questions that help create healthy relationships whether it's a family relationship, friendship, partnership or companionship.

Start Today

- ♦ Experience a transformation from the inside out
- ♦ Uncover your passion, promise and purpose
- ♦ Conquer limiting beliefs

Visit me at

www.transformbeyondthebreak.com

Message to the Reader

Thank you for reading this book. I hope you have enjoyed the journey thus far. The following *"Notes"* pages are to encourage you to apply some of the techniques you read about in this book. Having these pages readily available will allow you to track your progress as well as identify blind spots and road blocks that you may not have been aware of. Keeping notes will show you what works for you and what does not. It will also remind you of how you made it to your successes. A small success is still a success. Celebrate each one.

Notes

www.ingramcontent.com/pod-product-compliance
Lightning Source LLC
Chambersburg PA
CBHW062024040426

42447CB00010B/2133